ALL TIME HEROES

FROM ALL TIMES

~ Volume 4 ~

All Time Heroes from All Times

~ Volume 4 ~

The Coptic life of

Saint Pisentius

BY: JOHN THE ELDER

(Brit. Mus. MS. Oriental, No. 7026)

ST SHENOUDA'S MONASTERY

SYDNEY, AUSTRALIA

2015

All Time Heros from all Times - Volume 4
THE COPTIC LIFE OF SAINT PISENTIUS

COPYRIGHT © 2015

St. Shenouda Monastery

ST SHENOUDA MONASTERY
8419, Putty Rd,
Putty, NSW, 2330
Australia

www.stshenoudamonastery.org.au

ISBN 13: 978-0-9941910-3-8

Cover Design:
Hani Ghaly,
Begoury Graphics
begourygraphics@gmail.com

CONTENTS

INTRODUCTION

The life of our holy and glorious father, apa pisentius, bishop and anchorite in the mountain of tsenti, which john the presbyter narrated on the day of his commemoration, that is to say, on the thirteenth day of the month abib, in the peace of God. Amen.

The subject of this festival today is full of joy, for it is our holy father, who had put on Christ, Apa Pisentius, who was full light, and who spread abroad a sweet odour at all times, not only during the day, but during the night also. All the beasts which are upon the earth, and [all] the birds which are in the heavens rejoice, and move about gladly, and are happy this day because of the good and glorious news of him which has reached them, according to what the words shall inform us, if we are able to proceed to the end. I took an oath to keep silence and not to speak concerning your righteous acts and judgements, because you yourself did flee from the adulations of men from the very beginning, when you did become a monk, and before you became a bishop. Indeed if we were all to be gathered together, each one having the opportunity of speaking, one would declare [the greatness of] his knowledge, and another his power of disputation, and another would proclaim his power of revealing hidden things; and thus it would happen that all the descriptions [of him] would be laudatory.

Saint James the Apostle cried out in his Catholic Epistle, saying, "Him who knows to do good and does not do it, to him it is sin.' Let us learn, moreover, who it was to whom the Apostle [Paul] referred in his words, 'I know a man in Christ who fourteen years ago—whether in the body I do not know, or whether out of the body I do not know, God knows—such a one was caught up to the third heaven. And I know such a man—whether in the body or out of the body I do not know, God knows— how he was caught up into Paradise and heard inexpressible words, which it is not lawful for a man to utter.'

Of whom then was the Apostle speaking if it was not Pisentius? For all the saints have fled from the glory (or, adulation) of this world, and this did also our glorious father, Apa Pisentius, whom God has made manifest to us in our own days. He was a giver of light to the whole world. He was salt which was purified for everyone, according to that which is written in the Gospel, 'You are the salt of the earth; but if the salt loses its flavor, how shall it be seasoned?' And again, 'You are the light of the world.' He hid his life and the works thereof, but God has made manifest those who perform His will and commandments, generation after generation, according to that which is written, 'The Lord is near to all who call upon Him, to all who call upon Him in truth. He will fulfill the desire of those who fear Him; He also will hear their cry and save them.' Now if you wish to know whether he hated the glory (or, adulation) which was vain, and whether he wished not for any to applaud him in any way or not, let us know learn from him concerning the acts of his life and the manner in which he used to live and take heed to me with diligent attention.

THE PRAISE OF GOD
NOT OF MEN

It came to pass on a certain day, when he was still a monk, and before God had set him apart for the episcopacy, that he was meditating quietly by himself in the Mountain of Tsentê, when his brother came to visit him; now his brother was walking with a certain believing brother, and they met the holy ascetic face to face, and received a blessing from his holy hand. Then he asked them, saying, 'Have you any decided reason for coming into this region?' And they answered, saying, 'In the first place, we set out in order to come to you, and to pay you a visit, and to receive your blessing. For had it not been for the cares of the world which have occupied us for several days past we should have passed your way before this. In the second place, we have a little business in this neighbourhood which we wish to arrange; but you pray on our behalf, O father, that God may journey with us. If God be pleased to permit us to do this we shall return to you again, and we will salute (or, kiss) you, and receive your blessing before we return to our houses, if it be God's will.'

The holy man answered and said, 'Depart in gladness. But, O my sons, take good heed to yourselves, [and] do not commit sin. For neither the world, nor that which is in it, is of any account, because it exists for a season only. My sons, take good heed to yourselves in these villages. Hold no intercourse with a woman who is bad. Do not seize the ox of the poor. If there be any man in this region who is indebted to you, do not treat him harshly, and do not attempt to force him to pay by legal means; but watch what is in [his] mind, in order that God may show compassion to you.' And they answered, saying, 'Pray for us, O our father.' And they came away from his presence, and they acted [according to] his plan (or, way), and they gave glory to God because of the words of advice in which he had advised them.

The holy man, the anchorite, Apa Pisentius, stood up, and recited the beginning of the Book of Jeremiah the Prophet. Now [meanwhile] his brother, and the believing man who was travelling with him, departed, and they arranged their business according to the word of the holy man who had made supplication to God on their behalf. God made their way straight, and they returned to him in his cell in haste at the dawn of day.

When they had come to him, they heard him reciting the words of Saint Jeremiah with great calmness and clearness, and they sat down outside his place of abode for a little time, saying, 'It is not right, and the matter is not of such urgency as to make it seemly for us to cry out to the holy man inside until he has finished reciting the Scriptures and praying.' When Pisentius had concluded the reciting of the Prophet Jeremiah, and had finished [his prayer], the two men rose up and knocked at the door, at the very moment when he began to [recite] the [Book of the] Prophet Ezekiel. And they sat down, and did not cry out to Pisentius inside. Finally he finished reciting the whole of the [Book of] the Prophet [Ezekiel], and he shut his mouth, for the evening had come. When the two men knocked at the door, Pisentius answered them, saying, 'Bless me.' He looked out upon them from a large window, and he spoke to them, saying, 'Did you come to this place many hours ago?' And they said to him, 'We came here at dawn, but we did not dare to cry out to you inside until you had finished your recital [of the Scriptures].' Then straightway Apa Pisentins wept, and smote his breast, and said to them, 'This day I deserve a very great punishment, and all the labours which I have performed are things of vanity.'

Now these things which the holy man spoke [showed] that he fled from the vain adulations of men. He was very sad at heart, but the two men knew that he was reciting [the Books of Jeremiah and Ezekiel].

Know therefore, O my beloved, that the saints yearn for the glory of God only. If you will not [believe me], take heed to the psalmist David who said, 'I have desired Your commandments; look upon me and have compassion upon me.' And the truly wise man Paul cried out, saying, 'For in this we groan, earnestly desiring to be clothed with our habitation which is from heaven. And we have a building from God, a house not made with hands, eternal in the heavens.'

THE SAINTS COMFORT THE SERVANTS OF GOD

Take heed also to this great miracle which took place by his hands when he was a monk living in quiet contemplation in his cell and before he became a bishop. He was suffering from his spleen on one occasion on the third day of the festival at the end of Easter, but he did not make known to anyone of the brethren that he was sick, but he sent them a message and said, "Pray for me. I am going to the monastery of Apa Abraham to visit the brethren who are in that place. If the Lord be pleased to permit it I shall return to you." Now he spoke in this wise because he did not wish to let anyone know that he was seriously ill. Now if any man shall ask in a spirit of contentiousness why the holy man said this, let him read in the Book of Job the Blessed, and he will find that the Lord said to him, 'I have not done these things unto you for any other purpose except to make you show yourself to be righteous.' And Paul himself said, 'Now this I do for the gospel's sake, that I may be partaker of it with you.'

Now when the holy man Apa Pisentius had been sick for a whole week, and the brethren had made no enquiries after him, for they thought he was in a cave, they held converse with each other, saying, 'Pisentius tarries somewhat over long, let us enquire about him. Perhaps he has fallen sick on the road, or perhaps some suffering has afflicted him, and he is unable to walk.' They sent a brother who was a priest to make enquiries about him. Now when Pisentius had departed, according to the dispensation of God - now observe the wonderful acts of God - all the days which he had passed lying on his bed sick, during which the holy men did not minister unto him, until the very day wherein the brother went to him, the Lord sent His saints to visit Him. Now when the brother went to him, he found the door of the little cell wherein he lived open. And through the opportunity [afforded] by God, as soon as he had pulled the thong (or, latch-cord) of the door, he cried out [to the dweller] inside, according to the canon of the brethren, 'Bless me.' Now on that day it happened that Apa Elijah the Tishbite, he who belonged to Mount

Carmel, was with Apa Pisentius, and he was paying him a visit, having been sent to him by God in order to comfort him with his conversation. When the brother had waited for some time, he rose up and called out to [the dweller] inside, 'Bless me.' Then the Prophet rose up and was about to depart from him, but Apa Pisentius laid hold upon him, saying, 'I will not let you depart until I am comforted a little more.'

When the brother found that he was not able to obtain any answer to his greeting he went straight into [the cell], without any hesitation whatsoever, and he found there the two holy men sitting together; now Apa Pisentius was lying on his pallet, and Elijah was sitting by his side making enquiries concerning his health. When the brother had gone in he received a blessing from both of them and he stood still, but was wholly unable to look into the face of the Prophet Elijah, because of the rays of light which shot forth from his face like flashes of lightning, according to what is written, 'Then the righteous will shine forth as the sun in the kingdom of their Father.'

Then the holy man Apa Pisentius feigned to be angry with the brother, and he said to him, 'Is not this the commandment of the brethren - [not] to enter into [the cell of a brother] without permission? Had [this] been a governor would you have burst in upon him without permission from

him to you [to do so]?' The brother answered and said,
'Forgive me, O my father, I have sinned. Having waited
at the door for a very long time knocking, I thought that,
peradventure, you could not rise, and therefore I came
in to make enquiries concerning you.' Then the Prophet
answered, saying, 'This is an ordinance of God. In any case
he is worthy of our salutation of blessing, and because of his
righteous actions God will not deprive him of it.' When the
Prophet had said these things he went forth from the cell.

When he had gone out the brother spoke to Apa
Pisentius, saying, 'From where comes this brother who is
covered with hair, but who is surrounded with such a great
measure of grace? Indeed I have never seen anyone like him,
or anyone who was so gracious (or, gentle), or who was so
wholly filled with light. I say to you, my brother, that as soon
as ever I had grasped his hands and kissed them, mighty
strength came into my body, and I ceased to be without
power, and I became very strong indeed, and I felt as happy
as a man who had been tarrying in a wine tavern. I should
say that he must belong to this mountain, and yet I have
never seen anyone like him in our province, and I have never
seen any other man so hairy as this man.' Apa Pisentius said
to the brother, 'I say the same. You shall keep this matter
secret, and you shall not make known one word about it.'

The brother answered and said to Apa Pisentius, 'After a long time had passed, supposing that some necessity should come upon me, may I not reveal it? Why do you speak to me in this way? Will you not listen to Raphael, the angel who spoke with the holy man Tobit, saying, "The secret thing (or, mystery) of the king it is good to conceal; but the works of God it is good to publish abroad." Now I know that you hate the vainglory of men. Finally, but tell me in truth, who is this man, and I will trouble you no more.' And the thirteenth apostle Apa Pisentius answered and said to the brother, 'When I had departed from you, and was about to go to the brethren who are in the monastery of Apa Abraham, and to pay them a visit, I looked at my body and saw that it was powerless. I said, Will not a fainting sickness come upon me on the road? My spleen threw me into a sickness from the moment when I went away from you, and I never saw a man until you came to me [this day]. My spleen having continued to torture me most severely, I cried out to the Lord yesterday, asking Him to be graciously pleased to heal me. Now when He had seen my very weak condition, and my want of manhood, He sent one of the Saints to me, and was graciously pleased to grant me the healing of my body. And I say to you that this very man, from whom you did receive a blessing, is Elijah the Tishbite, who belongs to Mount Carmel. It was he who was taken up

into heaven in a chariot of fire and earthquake. I beseech
you, O my God-loving brother, not to reveal the mystery to
any man until the day of my visitation. Grieve not for me.'

Now when the brother had heard these things, great
joy came to him and consolation, and he did not reveal the
mystery to any man until the day when the God-loving
clergy of the Christ-loving city of Kebt (Coptos) laid hands
upon him that that was truly worthy of the episcopacy, that
they might take him to the Holy Patriarch Apa Damianus,
the Archbishop, so that he might consecrate him bishop.

Know then, O my beloved, that he that keeps the
commandments of monasticising, and fulfills them without
sluggishness, is loved by Christ. His holy ones do not speak
to Him only, but they see God, each one in the vision which
appears to him, according to the form wherein He wishes
to make Himself manifest to them. If it be not so [in your
opinion] take heed to the writings of the Spirit of God, and
they shall instruct you with divine knowledge according to
what is seemly, and according to the things which we have
said. For our Lord and Father and Bishop, Apa Pisentius,
whom God has made manifest in our time, is not the protector
of our district only, but of the whole country of Orthodox
Christians. But first of all come to the Book of Genesis, so

that we may see what it said concerning the seeing of God, and of what kind the vision is. Now as concerns Jacob the Patriarch, when Rebecca had heard the words of Esau, her eldest son, who was wroth with Jacob because of the blessing wherewith Isaac had blessed him, she cried out to him, and said to him, 'Behold your brother [Esau] is older than you, and the blessing which Isaac, who is your father, has blessed you [belongs to him]. Now therefore, arise, and flee into Mesopotamia of Syria, to Laban my brother, and abide with him until the fury of the wrath of your brother has turned away from you, lest peradventure I become childless in respect of both of you at once, and on the same day.' And Isaac also commanded him [thus], and he came out [to] Jacob and set him on his way, saying, 'Depart into Mesopotamia.' It came to pass that he arrived at a certain place, and stayed there all night, because the sun had set. And he took one of the stones of that place and put it at his head, and he lay down in that place to sleep. Then he dreamed, and behold, a ladder was set up on the earth, and its top reached to heaven; and there the angels of God were ascending and descending on it. Now God was standing above it, and He made Himself manifest to Jacob on that night, and He spoke with him.

Now when Jacob had gone into Mesopotamia of Syria, God spoke again with him in the night season, saying, 'Lift up your eyes and look with them, and you shall see that I will come to the white sheep, and the [white] sheep shall be with the goats, and they shall bring forth young of variegated colours, and they shall be in colour like ashes, and [some] sheep shall be marked with stars (i.e. spots).' Again God spoke to him in a vision of the night, saying, 'I am the God of Isaac; fear not. You shall certainly increase and multiply, and you shall fill the earth, and you shall become the lord thereof.' When God had blessed him with gold, and silver, and sheep, and goats, and cattle of every kind, He spoke again to him, saying, 'Return to the land of your fathers and to your family, and I will be with you.' Then Jacob returned with his two wives, Leah and Rachel, and their children, and their cattle. And when he had arrived at the river in order that he might pass over to the other side, according to the holy words of [the Book of] Genesis, which the holy prophet Moses wrote, 'A certain man met him, and wrestled with him until the breaking of day.' Now when the morning had come Jacob said to him, 'Tell me Your name.' The man said to him, 'Why is it that you ask about My name?' Now this is a most wonderful thing. The man said to Jacob, 'Let Me go, for the day breaks.' And Jacob said to him, 'I will not let You go unless You bless me.' And the man said to Jacob, 'What is your name?' And he said to him, 'Jacob.' The man said to Jacob, 'Your name shall no longer be called Jacob, but Israel; for you have struggled with God and with men, and have prevailed.' The man touched the side of a member of Jacob, and that member became without feeling. Then Jacob said, 'I have seen God face to face, and my life is preserved.' Now the sun was rising upon him when he passed .

O my beloved, it is right that for us this should suffice. If God deemed him worthy thereof, and came down into the world, and spoke to the creature which He had fashioned concerning his restoration with salvation of soul, how very much more will He not send His saints to comfort [His servants] in their sufferings? Therefore let no man allow himself to be unbelieving concerning this matter which I have related to him concerning the holy man Apa Pisentius the bishop, for he was worthy to see Elijah the Tishbite. And let not be fulfilled in him the words which are written, 'whose minds the god of this age has blinded, who do not believe, lest the light of the gospel of the glory of Christ, who is the image of God, should shine on them.' And again, 'Do not be unequally yoked together with unbelievers'; and again, 'The unbeliever is not [worth] one obolus.' Now our Lord Himself, and our God, and our Lord and our Saviour cried out in the Holy Gospel with His Divine mouth concerning the man who brought to Him his son. Now this son was possessed of an evil spirit, from the moment when his father begot him. And Jesus said, 'How long has this been happening to him?" And he said, "From childhood. And often he has thrown him both into the fire and into the water to destroy him. But if You can do anything, have compassion on us and help us." Jesus said to him, "If you can believe, all things are possible to him who believes." Immediately the father of the child cried out and said with tears, "Lord, I believe; help my unbelief!"' Then straightway [Jesus] rebuked the evil spirit, and cast him out from the young man because his father believed.

Again it was by the might of faith that a certain woman went to Him, whose blood had been flowing from her for twelve years, and whom no man had been able to heal. She touched only the outer edge of His garment, and immediately her blood ceased to flow, and dried up. Then He spoke to her, saying, 'your faith has made you well. Go in peace.' Again He spoke to the disciples, saying, 'if you have faith as a mustard seed, you will say to this mountain, 'move from here to there,' and it will move; and nothing will be impossible for you'. Again, you can say to this mulberry tree, be pulled up by the roots and be planted in the sea, and it would obey you.'

Before I Formed You In The Womb I Knew You

Moreover, it is said concerning the holy man Apa Pisentius, that it came to pass on a time when he was young, while he was pasturing his father's sheep, that God opened his eyes, and he saw a pillar of fire in front of him. Now there were certain other young men who were pasturing sheep with him. And he said to the other young men who were pasturing sheep with him, 'Do you see the pillar of fire on the road in front of us?' And they said to him, 'We do not see it.' Then he cried out up to heaven, saying, 'O God, open the eyes of these young men, so that they may see the pillar of fire even as I see it.' And God heard his voice, and the eyes of the young men were opened, and they saw the pillar of fire. And observe now, O my beloved, that the moment when

God chose Moses was when He spoke to him in his early manhood, out of a pillar of fire [which went up] out of a bush.

Now since God came to Apa Pisentius when he was a young man, He chose him even as He did Samuel, whose mother had given him to the temple of God according to her vow, even as the holy Psalmist says, 'Moses and Aaron were among His priests, And Samuel was among those who called upon His name; They called upon the Lord, and He answered them. He spoke to them in the cloudy pillar; They kept His testimonies and the ordinance He gave them.'

THE EFFECTIVE FERVENT PRAYER
OF A RIGHTEOUS MAN

Now there was in the Mountain of Tsentê a certain brother who was grievously sick, and his body was in a very weak and helpless condition because his sickness had lasted a very long time. It came to pass on a certain day that this brother longed greatly for a little fish, and he told the holy man Apa Pisentius about his longing (now at that time he was a monk, and had not yet become a bishop), saying, 'I long greatly for a little fish.' The holy man Apa Pisentius answered [and said to him], 'Assuredly God will give to you this day. Cast your burden on the Lord, and He shall sustain you, as the Prophet said; He shall never permit the righteous to be moved.' Then the holy man Apa Pisentius himself took his water-pot to fill it with water, for it was the time for filling [the water-pots with] water. As the holy man Apa Pisentius was walking along, he cried out to the Lord, saying, 'O God, permit not the heart of this brother to suffer grief, but, if it be Your Will, give to him his petition. Let him not suffer grief, O Lord.' When he had gone forth on the bank near the river to fill his water-pot — now the Nile flood was very high, for God had visited the country that year — Apa Pisentius looked, and he saw a large fish leaping about out of the water, and throwing itself about. O what a great miracle of God this was. At the very place where the blessed Apa Pisentius went to the river [to fill his water-pot], the fish came to the bank; now it was the current of the water flood and the force thereof which thrust it along and stranded it at that place. Whilst Apa Pisentius was filling his water-pot, according to what he confessed to us with his own mouth, and testified to us, he captured the fish, and [when] he gave it to the brother he said to him, 'God has fulfilled your petition; it was He who sent the meal to Daniel, for which his heart waited. He said, 'It is He moreover who has prepared the fish for you this day by His wish, inasmuch as He would not allow you to suffer grief in respect of that for which you did ask at His hand. Well and truly does the Prophet say, 'the Lord is near to all who call upon Him, to all who call upon Him in truth And He also will hear their cry and save them. The Lord preserves all who love Him.'

When the children of Israel had risen up against Moses and Aaron, they said to him, 'What is this that you have done with us? You have brought us forth from the land of Egypt. We used to sit down by the brazen pots of flesh, and we ate bread, and now the people have to be satisfied with manna instead of with loaves of bread and pieces of flesh. If not (i.e. if you do not give us bread and flesh) we will stone you.' The whole congregation spoke the word to stone them. Moses cried out to God, saying, 'O God, where shall I find to give to this people so that they may eat? Only a very little more and they will stone me.' God spoke to Moses, saying, 'I have heard the murmurings which the children of Israel have made against you. But command the children of Israel, saying, Prepare yourselves; tomorrow you shall eat flesh, not for two days, nor for three days, nor for ten days, but for a whole month of days shall you eat it, even until the flesh shall come forth from your nostrils.' And He brought over [quails] by a wind of the sea, two cubits upon the ground.

You must know, therefore, O my beloved, that the supplication of the righteous man is exceedingly powerful, and it avails much, even as it is written. Now as concerns Moses, the Lawgiver of the Old Covenant, immediately when he cried out to God concerning the multitude [of the Israelites], God did according to his wish. So also was it in the case of the Lawgiver of the New Covenant, Apa Pisentius. Immediately he made supplication to God on behalf of the brother who was a monk, God did not cause him grief, but fulfilled his petition, even according to that which is written in the Psalm, 'The Lord shall fulfill all your petitions.'

CALL TO ME AND I WILL SHOW YOU GREAT AND MIGHTY THINGS

Listen and pay attention moreover to the account of another great and wonderful thing which took place through the holy man Apa Pisentius, when he was a monk, and before he became a bishop. It came to pass on a certain day that he went to the well at which the brethren were in the habit of drinking, in order that he might fill his water-pot. Now when he had come to the mouth of the well, he [found that he] had forgotten the rope and the leather bucket, and had not brought them with him. When he had stood up at the mouth of the well he prayed to God according to the custom of the brethren, and he said, 'God, You know well that it is impossible for me to turn back again into the monastery to fetch the rope. Yet I pray command this water to rise up to where I am so that I may be able to fill my water-pot therewith, so that I may serve You for the remainder of my days. For You did command Your Apostle Peter, saying, 'Walk on the water.' Now when he had finished his prayer, the water rose in the well until it reached the mouth of the well, and he filled his water-pot with water. Then he said to the water, 'It is the Lord Who commands you: Go down again to your place.' Now while the water was sinking downwards, a certain shepherd who was pasturing his flock of sheep among the thorn bushes, directed his steps to the mouth of the well, and he looked in, and he saw the water going down by degrees until it reached its place at the bottom.

Unto whom shall I liken you, O blessed Apa Pisentius? Verily you are like Moses, the Lawgiver, who made the sea to be divided, one half being on this side, and the other on that, and the children of Israel walked in the midst of it as upon dry ground; and the water was to them a wall of water on this side and on that, on the right hand and on the left. It was Moses who spoke to the rock, and it sent forth fountains of water. As for you, O holy man Apa Pisentius, your prayer entered into the vault of heaven, and it fulfilled the Scripture, which says, "It was He Who spoke, and they came into being; for He commanded and they were created." You are a man of foresight like the Prophets, and a man of intellect like the

Apostles, and you are a wise steward. Therefore you were worthy of the Church of the Saints. God made you to keep alive a multitude of souls. You preached the Gospel like Paul, and you preached in wisdom the orthodox Faith. You did cry out in your discourse like a herald, you did shout aloud in your wisdom like a trumpet. Who is able to pay unto you the honour of which you are worthy, O just and holy man? For You knew the things which were hidden before they took place. Your discourse which appertained to the things of this world had therein songs and parables; your discourse which appertained to the monkish estate [was full of] spiritual explanations. Your words were those of a ruler, parables and mysteries. You never felt ashamed because of them before any man, according to that which is written, "I will speak of Your testimonies also before kings, and will not be ashamed." You guided those who came to you, all those who acted faithfully. You gathered together unto you everyone in the bond of love. You did take heed to the commandment of Christ, you built your house upon the rock which is holy. You brought forth fruit in patient endurance, and with a heart which is holy and good. You saw beforehand the Banquet of the Spirit, and because of this you now rest (or, recline) at the holy feast. You did seek out for the wretched the place where the pasture was good, and for this reason also you took care for the poor always.

You laid hold upon the ways of the ministry of God, and you were therefore a steersman in the sea of holy mysteries, and a saint like the Three Children. You were a father to multitudes of the poor in our time, and the father of those who were orphans in our days. You proclaimed like a herald peace to those who were afar off, O God-loving father, Apa Pisentius. You did exercise (or, train) those who drew near to you in the doctrine which was sound. You were a well-skilled spiritual merchant, and therefore you did bestow graciously your good gifts upon every one with great gladness and readiness. You sought and you did find, O God-loving father, Apa Pisentius, leader of the truth. You knocked and it was opened to you; you petitioned God, and He granted you all your petitions. There was great abundance in your days, and the Christians occupied great and honourable positions. The Church enjoyed abundance in your days and in your generation. Your people rejoiced in your wisdom, and your children rejoiced greatly in your holy mysteries. The Governors desired eagerly [to hear] your discourses, and all the proselytes sought eagerly after your mysteries. You looked upon the man whose name was Anatolês, therefore he filled you with the splendor of the Holy Spirit. You did complete the Ark of the Holy Spirit in its length and breadth, even as Noah [completed his ark]. You were a light which sent out its light into all our province.

Righteousness and peace made light your way before you all your days. Moreover, in your days lived two forerunners who sent forth light through your prayers, and through the prayers of the saints who lived in this province, that is to say, Apa Colluthus and Apa Paham, these [two] great saints!

Flee From Honour And It will Follow You

Now therefore, by the grace of God, we will tell you about another marvelous thing which I heard from certain men whose whole hope is the truth. Now a certain man from our district spoke to us concerning the holy man Apa Pisentius saying, "I went in and I received a blessing at his hands this day." Now when I had come forth from him, I met the holy man Apa Paham, who said to me, 'Have you received a blessing from the hand of Pisentius?' I said to him, 'Yes, my father, but you yourself are a holy man.' And he answered me, 'He who is truly a holy man is, most assuredly, Pisentius, and if you did happen to meet him you would have received a truly great blessing, for some time ago, when he prayed, the well became filled with water.' Now this man said to us, 'It came to pass on a certain day that we saw a fire burning in his house, and we said to each other, Is it possible that Pisentius has lit a fire? Why has he done this at this time of the year? And [some brethren] got up on the wall and looked over it, and they saw him standing up, and he was praying, and his hands were spread out towards heaven, and his ten fingers were like ten lamps (or, torches) of fire which were shining exceedingly brightly.'

Again, when God set him apart for consecration into the priesthood, of which he was worthy, because he loved the life of peaceful contemplation he went and hid himself. When the God-loving clergy were seeking him in order to make him take his seat upon the throne of the high priest, of which in very truth he was worthy, they sought for him a long time, and they found him at length in a secret place in the region of Djème. When they had caught him, he cried out and uttered the words of the great John, the Archbishop of Constantinople, saying, 'O the life of peaceful contemplation! I love it. Will you not leave me in it?' Finally they brought back the holy man, and they set him upon the holy episcopal throne. Now it was not he who ran in pursuit of the honour, but it was the honour which ran in pursuit of him, even as those who discovered him confessed to us, saying, 'He confessed thus to us with his own mouth: If it were not that I would not be disobedient to those whom you have sent after

me to this place, you might cut my head off me, or throw me
into the sea, before I would obey you, and forsake this life of
peaceful contemplation which God loves. Have you never read
what is written in the Psalms, 'Be still, and know that I am
God'? They debated the matter together, saying, 'Who then
is there that can command him [to accept]? It is not a man.'

Then they took counsel together, saying, 'Let us relate
the matter to the holy man Apa Colluthus, who is a great one
among men; he shall reveal the matter to him [in its true
light], and he will not hide the business from him.' And at
length they went to the holy man Apa Colluthus, and they said
to him, 'Father, when we had laid hold upon Apa Pisentius
in order that we might have him consecrated bishop, he did
not wish to bind himself, or to take any part in the service
of consecration. Behold, we went about very many days
seeking for him before we found him in a part of Djême.
When we had laid hold upon him he was most anxious to
excuse himself from his order. Afterwards he said, "If it were
not that I would not be disobedient to him that has sent you
to me, you might remove my head from me before I would
render obedience to you." We now therefore make appeal
to your holiness to abide with him for a number of days,
and do question him when you are alone with him, saying,
Who is he that has sent you? This matter is no miracle.'

Then the holy man Apa Colluthus questioned him, saying, 'The God-loving clergy [of the town of Coptos] state that your holiness said: "If it were not that I would not be disobedient to him that has sent you to me, I would not occupy this position [of bishop] at all." Now who are you [to speak thus]?' The holy man Apa Pisentius answered and said, 'Before the clergy came to my most unworthy self I fell asleep for a space, and a voice came to me three times, saying, "Pisentius, Pisentius, Pisentius. Behold the ordinance of the Church has come to you. Do not excuse yourself from the rank to which they would appoint you, which is that of Chief of the Apostles, but arise, and follow them. Do not forsake the Church, which is, as it were, a widow."

Now when I had heard these words, and when the clergy cried out to me in [my abode], I came forth, and I followed them, and I cast all my care upon Jesus, because nothing whatsoever can happen without [the consent of] God.'

Now, therefore, you must know, O my beloved, that that which I say to you is true, and that also which the wise man Paul said, 'Let no man takes this honor to himself, but he who is called by God.' When Aaron became high priest, it was not he who glorified himself, but He Who spoke with him, saying, 'You are a priest forever according to the order of Melchizedek.' Thus also was it in the case of the Christ, [for God said to Him], 'Today I have begotten You.' In this wise did Apa Pisentius take his seat upon the episcopal throne with a perfect [heart]. God gave grace to his face, even as to Joseph. No man dared to look into his face without being afraid of the fear of God which rested with him. Who could take into account the number of the acts of kindness and charity which he did to the poor, and not only to the needy folk of his own province, but also to those who came to him from a distance? He used to receive them himself, and give to them whatever they asked at his hands.

Deeds Of Mercy

You must know, moreover, that the praises which have been bestowed upon him are far too few, even for the early days of his episcopate, when he began to do acts of charity in every town and village [from Coptos] to Souan (Syene). The things (i. e. the offerings), which were brought to him year by year according to the Canons of the Apostles, he was accustomed to send secretly to certain men who were fearers of God in the various cities, and in the various villages, and they used to distribute it among the poor in the season of winter, when the poor are in the habit of lacking bread. He forgot the poor in nothing, even as you well know.

Now after a long time during which our holy Father Apa Pisentius had governed his flock with exceedingly great care, he dispatched [copies] of a letter to all the people who were in the province of Kebt (Coptos), and rebuked them, saying, 'Cease to do these great and grievous sins, concerning which we have been informed, lest perhaps God shall become wrathful with you, and shall deliver you over into the hands of the Barbarians who shall afflict you.' Moreover, he wrote also in that letter, saying, 'Unless you repent quickly, God shall bring that nation upon you without delay.' And again, after [this he wrote], 'Except you be instructed, that nation shall not cease to raise up wrath against you. [It is] a nation fierce of visage and cruel, and shameless in respect of its face; it shall neither spare, nor have compassion on old man or youth; it shall afflict you with sufferings which shall be as grievous as the plagues of Pharaoh of old, until finally he drove them into the abysses of the sea, thinking to destroy [them] openly. Therefore let repentance remain with you in your habitations at all times, so that it may be in your hearts, and let fasting increase in your mouth at all times. For charity shall boast itself over judgement, according to the word of James, the wise man of the Apostles.'

For the third angel in the salvation of God is the Angel of Charity. For charity shall deliver a man from death, and it will not permit him to go into the darkness. Moreover, it is very much better to perform acts of charity than to gather in gold. And you shall show compassion to him that is in debt to you. Let not your eye be envious of you whilst you do deeds of charity and righteousness. Moreover, it is better to give a very little with loving-kindness and righteousness than to give a great deal with violence. Do not turn your face away from any poor man, and God shall not turn away His face from you. Again, in respect of the little which one may owe you, be not afraid to give it in alms, even as the holy man Tobit said.

Consider the case of that rich man who despised Lazarus the poor man, and what was done to him in the matter of punishment, and how he answered and said in anguish of heart, 'Father Abraham, have mercy on me, and send Lazarus that he may dip the tip of his finger in water and cool my tongue; for I am tormented in this flame.' And what he heard was it not words of rebuke? For Abraham said to him, 'Son, remember that in your lifetime you received your good things, and likewise Lazarus evil things. And now he is comforted and you are tormented for your charity, for they will be as merciful to you as you have been to the poor. You fed yourself on young and tender flesh, and on small birds, and on other creatures, you ate by yourself the tender plants of the earth, you drank undiluted wine in glasses insatiably and without consideration for any other man. Concerning the man whom you did forget, and to whom you showed no charity with that which was yours, if there by chance remained to him the smallest amount of any possession, you were in the habit of demanding it from him unjustly. If you would not give to him of the things which were your own, at least you might have been kind to him, and watched and seen that justice was done to him; you should not have weighed him down with your injustice. For you know that you and the poor man were made of one and the same kind of clay. Do not give him cause to grieve, and God will not give you cause to grieve. There is a place of judgement wherein each man shall be judged according to what he has done, whether it be good, or whether it be evil.'

Cast Your Burden On The Lord And He Shall Sustain You

Behold, these are the things which the God-loving Father Apa Pisentius wrote on many occasions to all the people. Now how is it possible for us to beautify our encomium of the holy man, except by means of his own mouth? But let us invoke him, so that he may minister unto us in respect of the remainder of the things which it is seemly for us to narrate in this encomium, according to the measure of our inability. We are wholly unable to attain to the heights of your virtue, O good ascetic, who are adorned with the virtues of the Holy Spirit, [you doer of] all the righteous precepts and commandments which are full of life. Verily if every part of me was to become a tongue I should not be able to do honour to you in a manner suitable to the ten thousands of virtues which you possessed;

and moreover, as for the mite which we are able to cast into the treasury, it is your grace alone which has prepared it for us. For we know well that you have no need of our feeble tongue to utter these few words of encomium, because your citizenship is in the heavens, according to the words of the tongue of Paul, [who said], 'For our citizenship is in heaven, from which we also eagerly wait'. Nevertheless, let us declare a few things concerning the holy man, to the glory of God.

Now it came to pass that at the time when God brought the heathen, that is to say, the Persians , upon us, for our sins, Apa Pisentius departed to the mountain of Djême, and hid himself in that place because of the Persians. Now this took place at the time when the Persians were masters [of Egypt], though they had not as yet taken the city of Keht (Coptos). At that time, I John went with him, and I was with him in the capacity of a servant. Now I carried with me water-fillers and I put them in the place wherein we hid ourselves, so that we might be able to find them when we had need of them all the days which we should have to pass in hiding. Now, pay strict attention to the words [which I am about to say], for then you will marvel, and will give glory to God who performed these great and wonderful things by His holy man, even as God worked a miracle for Israel in times of old by Moses, to whom He said, 'Raise your rod, smite the rock, and the water shall gush forth so that the people may drink.' Now this was what happened in this case also. When he had departed to his hiding-place I myself went with him, and we remained in that place wherein we had hidden ourselves, and when we had passed several days in that place the very little water which remained to us came to an end, and I said to my father, 'We have no water left.' My father answered and said to me, 'God will not forsake us, O my son, but He will minister to all our wants. For He said, Do not worry about tomorrow, for tomorrow will worry about its own things. Again, at the time when Elijah the Tishbite was in the desert, the ravens brought bread to him every day in the early morning, and again at the time of evening. And when he had laid himself down and slept under the tree which is called "rathmen", and had risen up, he found there upon it a loaf of bread and a vessel of water. And an angel said to him, "Arise, eat bread, drink water." And Elijah ate the bread, and drank the water, and he journeyed on that road for forty days and forty nights, without eating any other bread or drinking any other water. Now God ministered to Elijah with spiritual food because he followed God with his whole heart; and we ourselves also shall be ministered to, if we observe His dispensations, and if our hearts be straight in respect of Him, He will take care for us. For He spoke by the holy Psalmist

David, saying, "Cast your burden on the Lord, And He shall sustain you." For God knows the things you have need of before you ask Him, even as He spoke in the Holy Gospel.'

Now when my father had said these things, he went away straightway. As for me I cast myself down on the ground, I heaped up the cool sand over my breast, I stretched myself out and lay at full length, and I was burning consumedly with heat, and the want of water. When my father had remained away from me for a very long time, he came back to me, and his eyes were full of light, like that of the luminaries in the heavens. His whole person was cheerful, and he was like one who had been in a wine-shop. He said to me, 'John, I see that you are exhausted by thirst, get to the waters, and drink.' And I answered and said to him, 'My father, the water-pots have been empty and dried up for the last three days, and there is no water at all in our place of abode.' Now my father used to fast three days at a time, and sometimes, when his body was free from sickness, he would fast even for a whole week at a time. Again he said to me, 'John, why do you not obey? Get to the waters, and drink, for I perceive that thirst is driving you wholly mad.' Again he said to me, 'John, be gone, for I see that you are greatly dried up through your thirst, and that you are mad through the darkness caused by want of water.' Then I answered him, saying, 'I did fall down, and I did go mad, and this is the truth, when you did depart into the desert; but now you have returned to me once more, and I perceive that your face is full of joy, and that bright light goes forth from it, even as from the face of Moses, the Lawgiver, the natural condition of my mind has returned to me, and I cease to thirst.' He answered and said to me, 'If you lose your reason in this manner after two days [of thirst], how very much more severe is the tribulation which has come upon those who are in the darkness of Amente, with the worm which never sleeps, and the outer darkness, and the river of fire which flows before the Righteous Judge, by whom we shall be tried! Verily, O my son, it is a fearful and terrible thing to fall into the hands of the Living God.'

When he had spoken these words he said to me, 'I think there is water in the water-vessels, in one of them which we have forgotten.' Now I, the wretched and miserable John, am not worthy to relate the wonderful thing which took place there, and which I myself saw with my own eyes; I the wretched man alone can narrate it. For when I had gone to the place wherein the water-vessels were - I confess to you, O my beloved, to [feeling] the doubt which would have come upon all of us - I found them filled with water up to their brims, and the water which was in them was as white as milk, and as white as snow, and was as sweet as the water of Gêôn (the Nile) which is in motion. Then I went and enquired of my father, saying, 'I found the water-pots full of water, from where comes the water then, O my Lord and father?' And he answered and said to me, 'He Who supplies with food the hawks which neither sow reap, nor gather grain into garners, He, I say, it is who has supplied us with these waters which we were in need. For him who casts his care upon Jesus, Jesus will care for him in every place, and He will serve him.'

Therefore, O my beloved, you must know that wherever a man goes, all his hope must be [set upon] Jesus. He must remember that which is written in [the Book of] Jeremiah the Prophet, 'Cursed is the man who trusts in man, but blessed is the man who trusts in the Lord, and whose hope is the Lord. He shall become like a tree which is planted by the waters, and his roots shall not perish for lack of moisture.' What shall I say, or with what words shall I describe all the glorious virtues of this glorious, and just, and blessed man? Now first of all I will declare concerning the manner in which he served God, and next concerning the grace which God bestowed upon him, and the gift which God most graciously endowed him, from the beginning of his life even to the end of it.

Unto Whom Shall We Liken You

Unto whom shall I compare you, O blessed man, Apa Pisentius? I will compare you to Abel who was the head of the worshipping of God and of the high-priesthood of God, and who became the first to offer up sacrifices and offerings. For this reason I ascribe blessing to your holy fatherhood, because you became a father to the orphans, and the mouth of the widow blesses you, O holy man and bishop, Apa Pisentius. You were a father to the weak and helpless, and a place of sojourning for the proselyte. You were food to those who suffered hunger, and water to those who were thirsty. You were apparel to those who were naked, and a garment for those whose nakedness was uncovered. You entered into Paradise in your understanding, and did eat of the tree of deathlessness. You were a wise man when you kept your mouth closed, and you were a man of understanding (or, discretion) when you did speak. For your name reached to the boundaries of the inhabited world.

You were a man of gracious speech concerning the wisdom of God, and you were a possessor of the true knowledge of the Holy Mysteries. You did seek first of all the Kingdom and its righteousness, and all these [other] things God graciously bestowed upon you. You entered into the land of promise in your mind, and therefore God gave you strength to vanquish the Canaanites who were hidden. You meditated upon all the spiritual paradigms, you understood all the parables of the Gospels, and you devoted yourself earnestly to the spiritual interpretations of it. All the wise folk that were in the land marvelled at your wisdom, and they had need of your advocacy in this world. And again the men who were learned in the knowledge of books marvelled at your wisdom, and all the men who were of senatorial rank were struck with wonder at your hidden sayings. For all those who were vexed in their minds came to you, and you, in the goodness of your disposition, gave them help. You were a righteous man in our days and a watcher in our generation, O holy man and bishop, Apa Pisentius, the blessed anchorite. In your days the Governors performed acts of loving kindness to the poor, and they gave glory to thy worship of God. You behaved like a nobleman towards those who drew near to you, and the Greeks ascribed glory to you. You made to be of no effect the office of the absolute ruler. You shut the mouths of the beasts, and the cages for prisoners in the prisons fell into disuse, and possessions returned to their rightful owners. You conquered Amalek like Joshua, the son of Nun, and you conquered the Amorite like Israel. You put on the whole armour of God, and therefore you were able to quench all the arrows of the evil one which blazed with fire, and you did do battle against all the crafts of the Devil. You laid hold on the breastplate of faith, and you put on your feet the preparation of the Gospel of peace. Your fame has reached to the boundaries of the inhabited world. You were a wise man in the opinion of Governors, even as was Saint Athanasius, and God gave you strength in the Scriptures. You did seek to know in your mind concerning the world which is to come, and you set out to examine into the depth of the wisdom of God, which is hidden.

You were a man inured to the contemplative life, even as was the holy man Apa Pahômô (Pachomius), the father of the coenobite life. God raised men to very high positions in your days, and in your generation He graciously bestowed upon us His peace. God brought forth your righteousness like the light, and He made your judgement to be like the hour of noon. You kept the commandments of God, and for this reason your peace was like to an overflowing river, and your righteousness like to the great and mighty deep.

Your spirit, which was mighty, was like the Morning Star, and your seed is like the sand which is on the sea-shore, which is without number. And your prayers, which were for the whole world, are in benevolent operation. You called to everyone to bring themselves to God in repentance. You taught the lawless man the ways of God, and you turned the impious men from their impiety. You raised up those who are sick by means of your holy prayers, and you cried out to God on behalf of those who were possessed of devils.

Unto whom shall I liken you, O blessed father Apa Pisentius, the holy bishop? You were a man who was a believer in our generation, and a man who was righteous in our days. You were a learned scribe in respect of your faculties, and a skilled reader of spiritual omens and portents. You were a master-physician who healed every one, with a benevolent heart. In the righteousness of God you did rise on high like a palm-tree, and you spread abroad in the wisdom of God like a plane-tree. You diffused abroad the sweet odour of virtue which was like unto [that of] cinnamon, and the sweet odour of your unguent reached even to the boundaries of the inhabited world. You were like the five cities in the gift of Christ, and the reports of all your marvellous works were in the city of the whole world. You were a teacher of rites and sacrifices like Moses, and a master of the art of making hymns like David. For we heard of your mysteries very frequently in your epistle[s], and we saw the depth of your understanding of the Holy Scriptures in the letters which you did indite, and of your wisdom which was great. You spread out your wings like the eagle, and you were transformed in the strength of the service of God like a young, strong eagle. God opened the eyes of your soul, and He taught you the gate of immortality like the Samaritan woman. Your understanding moved deftly in the perfect knowledge of the Scriptures, even as does the little stick in the hands of the player on the harp, and you did sing hymns thereby on a psaltery of ten strings.

Unto whom shall I liken you, O holy hermit, Apa Pisentius, the faithful priest? I will liken you to Noah, of whose holy sacrifice God smelled [the sweet savour]. For you did taste that the working was good, and your lamp was not extinguished during the whole night. You made for yourself celestial garments of byssus and purple, and you planted a vineyard of the fruit of your hand. You were a righteous man in the worshipping of God with all your heart and with all your soul. God gave to you rain from heaven as He did to Elijah. The things which were bitter He made sweet by means of your ministrations, even as did Elijah. The desert places became fertile in your days, and the hills poured out milk during your generation. You did build your children on the Rock which cannot be moved, that is the Christ, and you built in them the faith (or, belief) which is everlasting. You were the [place of] repose of the men of Egypt, and a kindly inn for those who were strangers. You became a sufferer in the service of the poor, and a help to those who were tortured with grief. You showed yourself perfect in spiritual knowledge. You did take your rest (or, die) in the midst of your children, like Jacob, and afterwards they followed you to your fathers, like David. You were a wise man like Solomon, and you did inherit the blessing from God. Because of this you did light upon the paths which were delicate, you made good your escape, you kept the faith, and you set the crown of righteousness upon your head.

You deposited seed for yourself in Zion, O Apa Pisentius, and you did beget for yourself a household in the Jerusalem of heaven. You received the sword of the Holy Spirit, through prayers of every kind and through supplications of every kind; and for this reason you were able to gain the mastery over the spirits of evil in the darkness.

You made yourself to resemble the Sun of righteousness in whose wings there is healing, and because of this the eyes of your soul sent forth rays of splendour. You did build a house for God, even as did Solomon, and you completed the courtyard of it as did Zerubbabel. You walked about in the meadow of the Spirit, and therefore you found in the treasury (or, field) holy mysteries. You were eager to receive in your heart, and therefore God gave you the star of the light of the knowledge of Him. You ate of heavenly bread, and you rejoiced yourself in the tree of immortality.

Unto whom then shall I liken you, O blessed man, the great priest, Apa Pisentius? I will liken you to Jacob, whom God remembered in his sufferings, because of his innocency, and gave him the inheritance. I will liken you also to Joseph, unto whom God gave a crown of the kingdom (i.e. a royal crown). I will liken you to Samuel, who [became master] of the gifts of grace of the high-priesthood. I will liken you to Samuel who became a priest, unto whom God gave the promise of the priesthood and of the office of prophet when he was a little child. I will liken you to the sons of Jonadab, who kept the commandments of their father. I will liken you to the Great Apostle, Saint Peter, who stood in an archi-episcopal rank. I will liken you also to Paul, who had the care of all the Churches. I will liken you also to Zacharias, the high-priest, whom God filled full of the Holy Spirit. For God gave you wisdom out of His mouth, even as He did to Solomon. You showed yourself to be like Moses, for God made the worship of idols to come to an end in your days, even as [in the days of] Ozias (Uzzah).

The man who went to you, no matter who he was, with a sorrowful heart, did he not come back rejoicing? O true consoler, according to the words of the Psalmist David, 'Your word has given me life, Your words comfort me.' Truly you are like Moses, whose face shone with glory, and who was exalted while God spoke with him. And you yourself, O Lawgiver, the similitude of your face was glorious through the strength of God which was with you. You were a companion of all the saints, because of the simplicity which was yours, and the purity which was yours, in the time when you were a monk, and before you received the honour of the episcopacy. Never at any time did any man who looked into your face feel fear of you, O you whose eye was full like the star of the morning and shot forth lightnings at all times. O blessed are the things which I have brought unto you! If I desired to narrate the account of all your successes I should be obliged to take to myself those who write down words (i. e. scribes), even as did Moses, the composer and establisher of the Law, until I had made manifest your valiant deeds, O holy and perfect man, Apa Pisentius. For you are like the holy anchorites Apa

Palamôn, and Apa Pahômô, and Apa Patrônios, and Apa Hôrsiesios, and Apa Theodore. You are like the holy man Basil, you are like Gregory the Theologian, each of whom was associated with the throne of priesthood like yourself.

THE SECRET OF THE LORD IS WITH THOSE WHO FEAR HIM

Now concerning the marvellous acts of your great power which were performed with quietness, no man whatsoever can know the full tale of them; but those which we have seen with our eyes, and those which we have heard with our ears that love discourses concerning his power, these, I say, are the things which we will now declare.

O you who are God-loving sons, know that [on one occasion] when the days of the festival of Easter drew near, now it was during the forty days [of Lent], the holy Archbishop of the Alexandrians sent messages to the South, throughout all Egypt, pointing out to the Bishops, and the clergy, and all the orthodox people, saying, 'Prepare yourselves, for, the days of

Easter are drawing near, and make arrangements concerning the forty holy days in respect of the months in which they are to fall, and the time when they are to come to an end.' The Patriarch Apa Damianus, Archbishop of Alexandria, despatched certain God-loving members of the clergy to the South with the holy message, so that they might deliver it in every city. Now it was the holy man Apa Damianus who had consecrated the holy man Apa Pisentius bishop of the city of Coptos. And when the God-loving clergy had arrived in order to sojourn with our holy father Apa Pisentius, they received a blessing from his holy hand, and they seated themselves in his presence. Now it happened according to the dispensation of God that on that day there were certain great men sitting with him. And a certain man who lived in a neighbouring country, who was a shepherd and was then pasturing his flock, came into the presence of Apa Pisentius that day, in order that he might receive a blessing at his hand. Now according to the favourable opportunity afforded by God, the shepherd came into the chamber as soon as he found that the door was opened, and he cast himself down at the feet of Apa Pisentius while the clergy who had been sent by the Patriarch Damianus were with him. And when he was standing upright, having kissed his holy feet, he brought himself near his holy hands so that he might receive a blessing, and he gazed in his face, and he wished to draw his hands to him. But the bishop would not give him the blessing, and he cried out, saying, 'Who is it that has permitted this worthless and sinful fellow to enter this place, who has allowed this man, whose head ought to be removed, [to come here?] Get gone out of this place, O you unclean one who are an abomination to God. Come here, John, and cast him forth.'

Then I John, the disciple of Apa Pisentius, laid hold of the man, and I cast him forth. When we had gone a little way outside the door, I enquired of him, saying, 'What have you been doing today to cause the great man to be so angry with you? Verily he passed the day very happily indeed, and was in a joyful mood until you entered his presence; his wrath would not have blazed up against you unless you had committed this day some very disgraceful deed. Besides this, the men of the Patriarch Damianus were sitting with him. Now, make confession to me, for it is written, 'Confess your trespasses to one another, and pray for one another, that you may be healed.'

The shepherd answered and said, 'How did it happen that I did not die this day when I rose up from my sleep? Now it came to pass that, while I was pasturing my sheep today among the thorn bushes, a woman passed me on the road whom I knew. I laid hold upon her in the foolishness of my heart, and I lay with her, thinking that the great man would never know anything about it. But, by God, who is the witness of my soul, immediately he looked at me, the consciousness sprang up in me that he knew what I had done. A mighty pain smote me at once in all my body, and I came near to falling on my face, and I should have done so if it had not been that you did seize me, and bring me out by the door. It (i.e. his look) mad me powerless, and I was about to fall upon my face.'

Then that shepherd brought several cheeses in wicker baskets, and he said to me, 'I entreat you to take these few cheeses from my hands, and to send them to these men who are with you in your house; since I have brought them, be not grieved at me.' Then I answered and said to him, 'I will not take them without the knowledge of the great man, lest if he find it out he scold me.' And that shepherd answered and said to me, 'I conjure you by God Almighty to take them from my hands, and to give them to the poor on my behalf'. Now when I heard [him mention] the awful (fearful) name of God, I felt afraid, and I took them from his hands on account of the oath [which he had sworn] by God. I carried them and put them down along with the other cheeses which had been brought to me that day. I said in my heart 'I will not let the great man know about my act at all.'

It came to pass at the hour of evening that day, that when the time for repose and meditation had come, he (i.e. Apa Pisentius) rose up in order that he might give some cheese to the clergy. He said to me, 'If cheeses have been brought to you this day, bring some of them here to me so that I may send them to the clergy of the Archbishop.' Then I took all the cheeses, and I threw those which the shepherd had brought with them. When the bishop had looked at them he said to me, 'Bring here to me a platter,' and he uttered the following riddle, saying thus: 'This day, a man whose eyes were open, a man whose eyes had no darkness [in them], and who saw clearly, covered up his eyes by day and by night, and walked about like a blind man, although his eyes possessed the faculty of sight. Would not every man who saw him rebuke him, saying, why is it since God has given light to your eyes that you love to adopt the guise of the blind men who walk in darkness at all times?' I confess to you that when my father had spoken these words to me, he picked out all the cheeses which the shepherd had given to me, and he divided them from the others, and placed them on the platter and said to me, 'I say to you that these cheeses belonged to the shepherd which I caused to be driven forth from me this day; now when you had thrown him out, why did you accept them from his hands? Look now, and consider; whom do you resemble? You resemble Gehazi, who ministered to Elisha, who made the man to turn back, and who took from him two talents and two changes of garments. Look now also and consider in what manner Elisha cursed him - he made the leprosy of Naaman to grow in his body. Now therefore, rise up, and take the cheeses to him wheresoever you can find him. Verily [even if you have to sit up] until midnight you shall not sleep in this place until you have given them to him.'

Then I said to Apa Pisentius, 'Forgive me, O my father. When I had thrown him out of the door, he swore mighty oaths to me, and I was afraid of the oath which he swore in [the Name of] God, and I took the cheeses from him.' And Apa Pisentius answered and said, 'Do not attempt to anoint my head with the oil of the sinner. It was Paul himself, who spoke in the Epistle which he wrote to the Corinthians saying, 'I wrote to you in my epistle not to keep company with sexually immoral people, and not even with anyone named a brother, if he is sexually immoral; have no friendship with him.' And again [he says]: 'fornicators and adulterers God will judge.' And again [he says]: 'Lest there be any fornicator or profane person like Esau.' And again it says: 'No fornicator shall inherit the kingdom of God.' Get gone therefore, at once, and give the cheeses back to him, and perhaps we may be able to deliver his soul from the hand of the Devil ; indeed he is a miserable man.' I departed therefore and I gave the cheeses to him on the evening of that same day, and I returned to my place according to the advice of my holy father.

Born Of The Spirit

Now you must know that our righteous father Apa Pisentius was inspired by the Holy Spirit, and he was a righteous man, and if [you imagine] that he was not, pay attention to the following narrative, and you will assuredly be struck with wonder.

Now it came to pass again on a certain day that my lord and father sent me on a message, which was urgent, to a certain district of Djême. Now it was very late in the day when I started to come back, and before I could get back it was dark night. When I had entered on the road which leads into [the mountain], behold, two hyenas came running after me, as I was riding my ass, and they sprang towards the ass wishing to seize her and to pull it down. In very truth their teeth were within a very little of touching my feet. And I cried out, saying, 'May the prayers of my father help me and keep me from the mouths of these beasts.' Before the words left my mouth, the animals took themselves off in another direction, and they did not do me the very least harm. Now by reason of the loudness of their panting it appeared to me as if they were fleeing in great haste from someone who was pursuing them; and they fled as soon as ever they heard the name of the great man, Apa Pisentius.

When I had journeyed on a little further, a number of wolves attacked me; now they ejected a lot of dung on my back, and threw up very much dust about me, and I was obliged to abandon the beast which I was riding. Again I cried out uttering prayers to God and to my holy father, Apa Pisentius, who had delivered me from the mouths of the hyenas, saying, 'Deliver me at this time also from these wolves.' Before the words had escaped from my mouth one of the wolves let out a mighty cry, and they all turned away and fled in another direction, through the prayers of my holy father, Apa Pisentius. [Now] they all turned away through the prayers of my father Apa Pisentius. Now as for me, I entered into the plain of the mountain of Tsentê, and I ascribed glory to God because of what had happened to me, namely that He had delivered me from the mouths of [these] evil beasts. When I had entered into the heart [of the mountain], I found her (i. e. the beast he had abandoned); and the holy man was engaged in studying [the book of a] certain prophet. Then I took the beast into the shed for the animals, and my father was looking down on me [as I did so] from the wall of the tower. And he said to me, 'O John'; and I made answer to him, saying, 'Bless me, my father!' And he said to me, 'Have I not told you that you are not to travel by the inner road late in the day, and that you are only to do so in the early morning? A very little more and the wild beasts would have eaten you up; they would have done so now had it not been for the mercy of God.'

Thus you may see, O my beloved, that he always knew what was happening, and no matter where the place was wherein any event happened, he was always certain to know about that event. But he kept it secret, according to the habit of his life, for he did not desire to give any man cause to give to him the approbation which appertained to men, even as the wise man Paul spoke, saying, 'Nor did we seek glory from men, either from you or from others.'

THERE IS NOTHING HIDDEN THAT WILL NOT BE REVEALED

Now, if I wished to tell you concerning all the works which we have seen done by the blessed old man Apa Pisentius, this discourse would become inordinately long, but inasmuch as the Scriptures inform us, saying, 'The works of God are good, make them manifest to everyone,' I will relate to you a few more deeds, out of a very large number, concerning the splendid acts of this perfect man, and afterwards we will bring our discourse to a close. Now it came to pass on a day that a certain man came to him from the district of Kebt (Coptos), and there was travelling with him his son, who had reached a time of life when he might, very properly, have been permitted to undergo the yoke of matrimony. The two men went together into the presence of [the holy man

Apa Pisentius], and they bowed low [before him], and cast themselves down at his feet. And the holy man said to the man, 'Why have you not taken a wife for your son? '- now that man was an inhabitant of the town of Coptos. The man answered and said, 'My father, he is a mere boy, and has not yet arrived at the proper age for marriage; and he is prudent.' The holy man answered and said, 'Verily your son is a habitual fornicator, and if you permit him, he will tell [you] the truth.'

The man said, 'If he be a fornicator, behold, I will put him into your hands, so that you may do to him whatsoever pleases you.' The holy prophet answered and said, 'When you go to enter into your village you shall meet a certain woman in the first street of your village, she is the daughter of such and such a man, and that which is inside her shall bear witness to you that it is your son who has been sleeping with her. But do not think that I say this wholly and solely of myself, most assuredly not, for I have been informed concerning this matter by certain men who are worthy to be believed. Nevertheless, if you will listen to me you will take her for him as a wife, inasmuch as he has humiliated her; and, in truth, I shall be unable to permit him to partake of the Mysteries until he has taken her as a wife. For the Law commands: "If a man finds a young woman who is a virgin, who is not betrothed, and he seizes her and lies with her, and they are found out, then the man who lay with her shall give to the young woman's father fifty shekels of silver, now fifty shekels is the proper price of a virgin, and she shall be his wife because he has humbled her, whether she be a poor maiden or whether she be a rich maiden."

'Now therefore, since the Devil made your son to fall in with the woman, depart, and take her for him as a wife. Do not give him the opportunity to commit sin, because God will enquire of you concerning the salvation of his soul. For if you will make him to enter into the estate of holy matrimony, and he fall afterwards into this sin, his blood by these means shall be on his own head, and on his only. Do not give him the chance of making you alone the excuse for his sin before the throne of the Christ, and of saying, "My father would not take a wife for me," for then the whole danger of his sin would be upon you, because you have taught him the Law of God carelessly, even as it is pointed out in the Holy Scriptures concerning Eli, the priest, saying, "He taught his sons the Law of God carelessly." Then the man answered and said, 'Every word which you have spoken I will truly keep, for he who shows himself disobedient to you shows himself disobedient towards the Christ, because the words which come forth from your mouth are the words of life.' Then the blessed Apa Pisentius said to him, 'The Lord be with you; depart in peace,' and they came away from his presence, and they did as he had commanded them, and their hearts enjoyed great rest.

SIGN OF THE CROSS

Again it came to pass on a day that our holy father Apa
Pisentius, the bishop, passed through the village to inspect his
churches. Now when he had finished he looked on them (i.e.
the people), and when he was returning to the monastery, and
was passing along the way by the canal, a certain husbandman
brought to him an ewe which belonged to him in order that
he might make the Sign of the Cross over her. Observe now
the power of God. The Sign of the Cross which the holy man
made on her with his finger sank down into her womb, and
when she brought forth her lamb they found on it the sign
of the Cross with which the holy man had marked her. Now
the holy man made the Sign of the Cross on the outside of the
ewe, and it appeared on the body of the lamb in the form of
a piece of white wool, which was like that of snow. And in
every man who was sick, no matter of what kind his sickness

might be, as soon as the holy man Apa Pisentius stretched out his hand over him, and made the Sign of the Cross over him, the sickness ceased. Come then, O all you whose hearts are straight in respect of God and the holy man, and let us make supplication to him with tears and with repentance, in order that Apa Pisentius may entreat the Christ to show mercy upon us when it shall come to us to meet Him face to face; for it is a fearful thing to fall into the hands of the Living God.

ALL THINGS ARE POSSIBLE TO
THOSE WHO BELIEVE...

Now if there be among you anyone who shall be so
bold as to waste his time in trying to refute the statement
which I have dared to make to the effect that the holy man,
Apa Pisentius, the bishop, is a companion of the Christ, let
him come now and consider the words which are in the
holy Gospel according to John, and let him hear God crying
out by the mouth of His holy and beloved one John, the
Evangelist, saying, 'You are My friends if you do whatever
I command you.' And again, 'I have called you friends,
for all things that I heard from My Father I have made
known to you.' And again, 'You did not choose Me, but I
chose you and appointed you that you should go and bear
fruit, and that your fruit should remain.' Know therefore,

O my beloved, that he who does the will of God, the same is His companion and His friend, even according to what is said in the holy Gospel, 'For whoever does the will of My Father in heaven is My brother and sister and mother.'

It came to pass on a day that they brought to him a certain youth who was possessed of a demon, and they implored the holy man, saying, 'Do an act of gracious goodness, and be pleased to make the Sign of the Cross over him, for the demon which possesses him is exceedingly evil.' The holy man asked his father, saying, 'Did this calamity come upon him a very long time ago?' And the father of the youth said to him, 'Behold, it is seven years, [since we have asked] your prayers, O my father. The demon is in the habit of casting him on the ground, and of making him to stagger about like a camel, his eyes being filled with blood, and often and often this has continued until we were in despair of him, thinking that the demon would kill him. And [sometimes] he does not speak at all. Do an act of gracious goodness, and be pleased to help him, O my father.'

Then my father cried out to me, 'John ' and he said to me, 'Go to the laver of the congregation, and bring here to me a little water, so that I may sprinkle it upon this youth, for I cannot endure seeing this demon inflicting such severe suffering upon him.' I went therefore into the room of the assembly, according to the command of my lord and father, the blessed Apa Pisentius, and I made Apa Elisha, the presbyter and overseer of the place (or, shrine), go into the place of the altar of sacrifice, and he poured a little of the water which was there into a vessel, and I brought it to the holy man; and the holy man dipped his finger in this water, and made the Sign of the Cross on the youth in the Name of the Father, and of the Son, and of the Holy Spirit. He gave some of the water to his father, saying to him, 'Take your son, and depart to your house, and you shall give him to drink of this water which I have given you from the laver of the congregation, and you shall believe in the Lord, and He shall heal him.'

Now, my father acted in this way and did not himself give the youth the water to drink with his own hands, and so make the demon come out from him immediately, lest men should ascribe praise to him, and say, Apa Pisentius has cast the demon out of the son of such and such a man, because he did not wish to receive glorifying from the children of men.

It came to pass that when the man had taken his son, that he might depart to his house, now, according to what the man himself confessed to me with his own mouth, [this happened] a few days after, while he was taking him back home, [and the man said], 'While I was walking along with my son, and when I was a long way from you, the demon suddenly hurled him to the ground, and made him writhe in agony, and then cried out inside him, "Pisentius, by the Sign of the Cross which you made with your finger, you have driven me forth from my dwelling-place." Immediately when the youth was purified I took him into my house with joy, and the demon never returned to him to the day of his death.'

It came to pass that after a few days, the [father of the youth] went to the great man, and he made obeisance to him, and he laid hold of his hand, saying, 'I tell you that the young man is free from the demon.' The father of the youth confessed to him, saying, 'I tell you, O my father, that immediately I had given him to drink of that water which your fatherhood gave to me, the merciful Lord graciously bestowed healing upon my son through your holy prayers.' Apa Pisentius answered, saying, 'Everything is possible to him that believes; and assuredly the water which is in the chamber of the altar of sacrifice heals everyone who believes. Do not think that this gracious healing is to be attributed to me, for assuredly it is in no way whatsoever due to me, but to the power of God which abides in His holy shrine, and is given to those who enter therein in sincere faith and with a heart where there is no unbelief. As for me, O my son, I am the least of anything in a matter of this kind.' When Apa Pisentius had said these words, the man departed from his presence, and ascribed glory to God, and rendered abundant thanks to my blessed father.

GOD LOOKS AT THE HEART

Again it came to pass on a day that the spirit of jealousy invaded the heart of a certain man, and he became jealous of his wife. The Devil, the hater of that which is good, and who longs to do evil to the race of mankind, cast a stumbling-block into the heart of her husband in respect of a man whom he believed to have had carnal intercourse with his wife. Now the woman was innocent of that offence, and the man who was accused was himself innocent of the charge of impurity which was brought against him in respect of the woman, even as the story itself will teach us if we proceed with it to the end. So the husband cast out his wife from his house because of the evil which existed in his own heart in respect of her. His father and his mother both took the greatest pains, but were wholly unable to convince the mind of the husband [of his wife's innocence], and to make him to live with her;

even according to that which Solomon spoke, 'The heart of her husband is full of jealousy'. Finally the matter came to the ears of the clergy of his village, who had made him an assistant in the administration of the Holy Mysteries, and the clergy informed my holy father concerning the matter. Then my father sent a message to him, saying, 'Trouble [not] yourself: I will find for you the defence which is necessary.' The husband spread abroad rumours throughout the village, and he went about from place to place threatening, and saying, 'I will never again go to Pisentius; what has Pisentius to do with my affair?' Now the man was a native of the town of Kebt (Coptos). And during the time in which he was uttering [these] words he became more and more angry.

When the sun was about to depart to its place of sunset on that same day - now it was God who said in [the Book of] the Prophet, 'Cast [your] dispute upon Me, I will avenge you,' says the Lord -a certain terrible sickness came upon that man with the darkness, and he began to suffer great tortures in his inward parts, which caused him intense pain, and he cried out with a loud voice, saying, 'Take me to my father Apa Pisentius, for I tell you that [these] pains have come upon me through him. O my father, do a loving act, and help me, for indeed I have come into the straits of death (i. e. to the last gasp). And if you do not take me to him, I shall never find relief.'

His father and his mother despaired [of his life], and thought that he would die. They said, 'Since he says "Take me to Apa Pisentius, the bishop", if he is to live, let us persuade ourselves to do as he says. In any case, if we take him to him, and he make the sign of the Cross over him, at least the tortures which he is suffering will be lessened.' Now this took place very soon after my father Apa Pisentius had been made a bishop.

Then they took the sick man up to the mountain to my father, and they called out inside [the court], and I [John] went out to them. The father of the man said to me, 'John, if you would ever look upon me again, do an act of love, and inform the great man, for if you do not my son is in danger of dying, and I believe by God, that if he were to make the sign of the Cross over my son he would find relief immediately. He has entreated me, saying, "Take me to Apa Pisentius, the bishop, in order that I may have relief from these pains by which, through his agency, I am suffering torture." Now if I were to discuss the matter with the bishop in my present distracted state, I should talk like a man without understanding.' His son also cried out to me, saying, 'O John, do an act of love, take in the news of my arrival to the great man, for the straits of death have come upon me. Behold you see me yourself in my necessity. O why did I not keep my mouth shut, and why did I not die before I repeated the report that day? Get in quickly, and inform my lord and father Apa Pisentius about my sufferings. Help me, and do not abandon me to death on your threshold.'

When I had heard these things from the man and from his son, I went in and informed my father concerning [the arrival of] the man and his son, And he said to me, 'Keep away from him until he makes the petition in a proper manner, for he is not a man without education.' I answered and said to him, 'If I leave him outside a very little longer, he will die. The breath which is left in him at this moment is very little, and according to what I see of him he has contracted a fatal disease.' Then my father said to me, 'Let him [enter] in with you.' And when he had come in with his father, he threw himself down at the feet of my father, and remained there for a long time. My father said to him, 'Rise up, O boorish man.' And the man answered and said, 'As the Lord lives, if I have to pass three whole days kneeling at your feet I will do so; unless you lift up your feet on my head, I will not rise up.' My father laid hold upon the hair of his head, and lifted him up, and he said to him, 'Rise up, for behold God will bestow healing upon you graciously, if only you will listen to me.' The man answered and said, 'I swear by my necessity in which your prayers have delivered me, that whether I live one year [more] or two, I will never, never again dare to be disobedient to you.'

My father answered and said to him, 'What I have to lay upon you is this – You have driven your wife out of your house for no reason whatsoever. And as concerned the offence with which you have charged her in your mind, she and the man also are both innocent. But I say to you, supposing that you wish to be wholly satisfied in respect of her, and in respect of the man of whom you have thought evil in your mind - now, my son, man looks at the face only, but God looks at the heart - when you go into your house, take your wife back into the house, and God shall make you to be acceptable to her, and if she shall incline to you, and shall conceive and bring forth a son to you, [you will know that] the report which has been spread abroad about her is not true. And believe me, for she is a free woman. If, however, she shall bear you a daughter, live not with her, but cast her forth from your house, for she is not innocent of the offence with which they have charged her, and she has defiled her marriage [bed]. But if it be a son which she shall bring forth, the report which has been spread abroad about her is not true, and she is innocent of the charge of which she was thought to be guilty. If you wish to make her swear an oath I shall not attempt to prevent you, for the law of God gives the following command: "If the wife of any man goes astray and behaves unfaithfully toward him, and a man lies with her carnally, and it is hidden from the eyes of her husband, and it is concealed that she has defiled herself, and there was no witness against her, nor was she caught, the woman shall be taken to the priest, and he shall make her take the oath, and he shall give her the water of the curse, and she shall drink it. If the offence with which she is charged has been actually committed, that water shall make her body to become covered with burning pustules [and] leprosy. But if it be that she has been accused falsely, she shall conceive a son." And now, O my son, if you are quite satisfied about the matter, [good and well]; but if not, make her take the oath. I shall not attempt to prevent you.'

The man answered and said, 'From that very moment when your fatherhood [began] to speak to me my heart has been satisfied about the matter. And I shall never again hesitate to obey you.' And he received a blessing from the holy man, and he came forth from his presence and departed to his house with his father, glorifying God and the holy man Apa Pisentius. Now when he had gone into his house, he made peace with his wife, and begot a son according to the word of Apa Pisentius, who was like an Apostle. And the man called the name of his son 'Pisentius', and he lived with his wife from that very day until the day of his death. And the holy man performed three miracles, each of which was more wonderful than the other, and these are they; [the miracle] of the woman whom he delivered from the false accusation in which she had been charged; and [the miracle] of the man who was made a free man; and the setting free of the body of the husband of a woman, on whose navel a spell had been cast by the power of Satan, and the making of those who had been married to live together in peace again.

Verily, exceedingly great is you wonderful life, O angel of the Lord of Might! For who is able to recount all the wonderful things which have taken place through you, both those which belong to the period of your youth (or, childhood), and those which have taken place during the time in which you lead the life of a monk? And as for those which took place through your hands after you became bishop, and which you did order, and wished that no man should ever gain any knowledge of them whatsoever, no man could possibly describe them completely. Now you must not make the soul of the blessed man to condemn me because I have related these few matters in [my] Encomium upon him, for I think that we have not exceeded the measure in declaring merely these few unimportant matters. But let us take heed to the following commandment with which the Apostle commanded us, saying, 'Render therefore to all their due: taxes to whom taxes are due, customs to whom customs, fear to whom fear, honor to whom honor.' Verily, [O Apa Pisentius,] you are worthy of all honour and all glory, according to that which the Psalmist David says, 'Give unto the Lord glory and strength. Give unto the Lord the glory due to His name.'

Now pay attention to another great and wonderful thing, and ascribe glory to the Lord! And it came to pass on another occasion that a certain man came to him, and made supplication to him, saying, 'I beseech you to perform an act of love, and to help me, O my lord and father. There is an obligation on me in respect of a certain man of thirty-six "holokottinoi", and they are pressing me urgently concerning them, and I am not able to find them to pay them to him. I possess nothing whatsoever except a son, my only son, and him they have seized, and they have put him securely in the guard-house (i. e. prison), and they are wishing to make him a slave. I beseech your fatherhood to show compassion upon me. If there is anyone whom you could cause to give me this small sum I could go and give it to the man, and then they would let my only son go free.' Now that man was a soldier, and he was a native of the district, and he dwelt in a part of the mountain of Teiladj. Having heard of the fame of my father, and that he was a most charitable and generous bishop, he rose up and came to him with his wife, and he wished to find out whether he was one who gave alms freely or not. Now he put the woman again into the boat in which he brought her, and he hid thirty-six "holokottinoi" in the boat with her; now these he had carried off from a man whose blood he had shed.

He came to my father wishing to try him and to see whether that which he had heard about him was true or not. Now the day where he came to the holy bishop Apa Pisentius was that in which the bishop had gone into the holy congregation of Tsentei, and had taken part in the Catholic Synaxis, for it was the day of the festival of the Archbishop and Patriarch, Apa Severus, Archbishop of Antioch. He sat down until Apa Pisentius came out from the congregation, when he cast himself down at his feet, and informed him of the matter that which I have already spoken.

When the great man had heard it, he said to the soldier through an interpreter, 'The place of Pisentius is not a place for jesting. Get gone, and take the thirty six "holokottinoi" from the hand of your wife who is on board the boat by the place of the ferry. As for the money, behold, it is tied up in a bundle in her hand, and it is this which you have brought to tempt me with. Behold now what it was that you wished to do. Because you have shed the blood of a man, and have taken [these moneys] out of his hand, you did say, "I will take them and give them as an offering for the salvation of my soul." Verily I say to you, that if the whole world were

given in alms on your behalf then the smallest act of mercy
shall never be shown to you, until your own blood has been
poured out even as you have poured out the blood of your
neighbour, according to that which is written, 'Whoever
sheds man's blood, by man his blood shall be shed; For in
the image of God He made man.' Now when the man had
heard these words he marvelled exceedingly, for he thought
that the matter would be hidden from the new Elisha, and
he did not know that the Spirit which spoke to the Apostles
was the same as that which spoke in the Prophets, and he
did not know that the God was the God of all of them. And
he came forth from the presence of Apa Pisentius weeping,
and he went into his house exceedingly sorrowful at heart.

Because He Has Set His Love Upon Me

Now you know, [O my beloved,] that in the beginning of this Encomium I did not fail to say that the blessed man Apa Pisentius was endowed with the gift of the Spirit, for whenever any man went into his presence, as soon as he had looked into his face he knew for what purpose he had come to him. But he hated the vain approbation of men, and he hid his manner of life so that no man whatsoever might attain to the full knowledge of the same.

Now it came to pass also on another occasion when he was fleeing from before the face of the Persians [that] he might lead a life of peaceful meditation in the mountain of Djême, that he departed into the mountain not a little way in order that he might pray. When he had passed three or four hours in travelling, he prayed in place after place, and there is no man who is able to estimate the number of the prayers which he made by day and by night. Now, he was in the habit of praying four hundred times during the night. He turned to me, and he said to me, 'Take good heed to yourself for I found a huge serpent in the mountain today; and he is not very far from us at this moment. But I have confidence in God that He will not permit him to remain in our neighbourhood.' Now when the morning had come, I looked out, and at the distance of about the flight of an arrow, I saw a very large number of birds and vultures gathered together upon a crag of the rock. And [my father] cried out to me, and said to me, 'I think that God has destroyed the dragon.' He spoke yet again to me and said, 'Why have you not given your attention to the words of the Scriptures, and understood them, according to that which the wise man David says: Because you have made the Lord, who is my refuge, even the Most High, your dwelling place, no evil shall befall you, nor shall any plague come near your dwelling; You shall tread upon the lion and the cobra, the young lion and the serpent you shall trample underfoot; Because he has set his love upon Me, therefore I will deliver him; I will set him on high, because he has known My name. He shall call upon Me, and I will answer him.'

GREAT IS YOUR FAITH

It came to pass on a certain day, according to the will of God, that he went forth, and came to the well in order to fill his water-pot with water. And he walked back, and as he was about to enter his cell he met two women who were seated by the path and were in sorrow. As soon as they saw him, they rose up, and ran after him to receive his blessing, and to kiss his holy hands. Now one woman had a violent pain in her head, and she was suffering so much down one side of her face that her eye projected from its socket, and seemed as if it was about to fall out; the other woman was dropsical and her whole body was swollen. When the holy man saw that they were gazing intently upon him, he covered his head with his cowl and casting his pitcher of water on the ground he fled. The dropsical woman sank down on the path, for she was unable to run after him. And the holy man cried out, saying, 'Why do you run after me? O wrath, where shall I go this day? Get away from me, depart!' The woman said to him, 'My father, I am ill, I suffer pain through my scourge, I beseech you to stand still and to lay your holy hands upon my head; I believe healing will come to me.' He said to her, 'And what power can there be in my littleness? Go to the brethren, and they shall pray over you, and you shall be healed. For as for me, I am a miserable sinner.' Meanwhile he did not stop running until he had entered his cell and shut the door. And the woman who had the pain in her head said, 'Although I am not worthy to kiss your holy hands, O my father – now he knows that I am unworthy to touch him because of the multitude of my sins which I have committed – I may at least – she said – carry away a little of the sand from the place where he has set his holy feet, for it may be that in some way or another the Lord will graciously bestow upon me healing through his holy prayers.' The woman, by reason of the great faith which she had in him, carefully marked the places where the right foot of the holy man Abba Pisentius had fallen, and she took the sand from there, and placed it in her cloak, and she lifted it up to her forehead, and said, 'In the Name of the Father, and of the Son, and of the Holy Spirit, graciously grant healing to me through the prayers of my holy father Abba Pisentius.' Straightway the pain in her head ceased, and she walked along ascribing glory to God through the prayers of our father Abba Pisentius. When she had come [back] to the place where the dropsical woman was lying upon the ground, she said to her, 'Did you reach the holy man? Did you receive a blessing at his hands? If your hands have touched his holy hands, lay them upon me; I believe that I shall have relief from the whip of this disease which is upon me.' And the [other] woman said to her, 'He did not lay his hand upon me. He ran away until he came to his cell, and he went into it and shut the door. And when I saw that I could not overtake him, I took the sand which had been under his right foot, and I lifted it up on my head, and by the grace of God, I had relief from my sickness.' The dropsical woman through her great faith said, 'Give me also a little of that sand.' And she took it, and swallowed some of it, and it entered into her body, and her belly, which was swollen, subsided, and her whole body was healed. And they carried the [rest of the] sand to their houses, and laid it up in there as a blessing for them. After these things the woman who had had the pain in the head, who had a little son who was slow to grow, and he could neither walk nor speak, and who had laid up the sand of the holy man in her house – O the miracles of God, Who exalts His chosen ones, and makes them manifest – this woman [I say,] took some of the sand,

and threw it into water, and washed the child with it, and made him drink some of it. And the parents of this child have testified to me that not a week had passed before his feet were made straight, and he walked well, and the string of his tongue was loosed, and he spoke like all other people.

Make Confession
To The Lord

One day he looked and he saw an elder shoot spittle from his mouth in the sanctuary, while the Mysteries were being administered to the people. And straightway he caused them to call him to him in the place where he took his rest. The holy man Abba Pisentius said to the elder, 'My son, what is this audacious act which you have committed? You have spat in the holy place. Show me what you have said in your prayer. Do you not know that there are tens of thousands and tens of thousands of Angels, and Archangels, and Cherubim, and Seraphim standing close to you by the altar, and saying with one voice these beautiful words, "You are holy, You are holy, You are holy, O Lord of Hosts! Heaven and earth are full of Your glory"? Do you not know who these are who are standing here? Believe me, my son, another priest spat, as you did, in the sanctuary, and he came away and died.' And it happened that a brother who was a monk came to us to visit us from the Eve of the Sabbath to the dawn of Sunday, and he was an elder. And as we had charge of the altar we ordered that elder to perform the Offering. And he said the prayers until he came to the place where he should invoke the Holy Spirit to descend upon the Bread and the Chalice [without difficulty], but at that place he was seized with coughing, and he spat. Straightway he became dumb, and he was unable to speak at all, and immediately he died. And I gave the order to another elder, whose name was Eliseos, to finish the Offering, and we received the Holy Mysteries. When we had dismissed the assembly the brethren entreated me to pray for him that his heart might be quieted. And I prayed for him, saying, 'O Lord God Almighty, the Father of our Lord Jesus Christ, You know, O Lord, that the nature of mankind is perishable, make the heart of this brother to return to him so that he may inform us as to what has happened to him, in order that we may take good heed to ourselves for the rest of our days.' While I was making my supplication to the Lord, a voice came to me, saying, 'Through your prayers, behold, I open his mouth so that he may tell you what happened to him. Ask your questions of him quickly, for behold his sentence has gone forth from the Lord, and behold, the angels have drawn near to carry away his soul.' In truth when I heard these words fear seized me, and great affliction of heart came upon me, and I became like a man in the sea, with the waves casting me from side to side. At length I began to speak to him, and I said, 'My son, O elder, what is it that you did this day [which caused] this great matter to come upon you? Make known your sin, for the Lord is compassionate.' The elder answered – now his body trembled through fear – and said, 'O my lord and father, entreat the Lord for my sake in order that I may find mercy. I swear by the fear which has come upon me this day that I know of nothing which I have done except that a fit of coughing seized me, like [an ordinary] man, that phlegm came to me, and that I spat it out. What it fell upon I do not know. [Then] a little feather touched my ear, and I turned my face behind me. When you prayed for me, it was given to me to speak to you.' And I said to him, 'In truth, my son, there are many men who are men by nature, but who are like the beasts, and do not know what manner of beings they are. Instead of thinking about that which comes forth from your mouth, it is for you to order your life well, and to remember the word of the prophet which says, "Nevertheless man, though in honor, does not remain; he is like the beasts that perish." And as for you, you did stand by the table, you did spit, and your spittle reached the wing of a Cherubim, who overthrew you with his wing, and I think that your sentence of doom has gone forth.' When he had explained these things to me, I spoke to him the words [given] above. Then straightway he sent for his men, and they set him upon an ass, and they carried him to his house; and on the third day he died.

The God Of The Living
& The Dead

It came to pass on a day while my father was still with me in the mountain of Tjêmi that my father said to me, 'John, my son, rise up, follow me, and I will show you the place where I repose and pray so that you may visit me every Sabbath and bring me a little food, and a little water to drink with which to support my body.' My father rose up, and walked before me, and he was meditating on the Holy Scriptures of God. When we had walked about three miles, at least so the distance appeared to me, we came to a path which was in the form of a door which was wide open. When we had gone inside that place, we found that it had the appearance of being hewn out of the rock, and there were six pilasters rising up against the rock. It was fifty-two cubits in length, it was four-cornered, and its height was in proportion [to its length and breadth]. There was a large number of bodies which had been mummified in it, and if you were to merely walk outside that place you would be able to smell the 'sweet smell' (i.e. spices), which emanated from these bodies. And we took the coffins, we piled them up one on top of the other – now the place was very spacious. The swathings where the first mummy, which was near the door, was wrapped, were of the silk of kings. His stature was large, and the fingers of his hands and his toes were bandaged separately. My father said, 'How many years ago is it since these [people] died? And from what nomes do they come?' And I said to him, 'It is God [only] who knows.' And my father said to me, 'Get going, my son. Sit in the monastery, take heed to yourself, this world is a thing of vanity, and we may be removed from it at any moment. Take care for your wretched state. Continue your fastings scrupulously. Pray your prayers regularly hour by hour, even as I have taught you, and do not come here except on the Sabbath.' When he had said these things to me, I was about to come forth from his presence, when looking carefully on one of the pilasters, I found a small parchment roll. When my father had unrolled it, he read it, and he found written in it the names of all the people who were buried in that place; he gave it to me and I put it down in its place.

I saluted my father, and I went away from him, and I walked on, and as he showed me the way he said to me, 'Be diligent in the work of God so that He may show mercy to your wretched soul. You see these mummies; surely everyone shall become like them. Some are now in Amenti, - those whose sins are many, others are in the Outer Darkness, and others are in pits and basins which are filled with fire, and others are in the Amenti which is below, and others are in the river of fire, where up to this present time they have found no rest. Similarly others are in a place of rest, according to their good works. When a man goes forth from this world, what is past is past.' When he had said these things to me, he said, 'Pray for me also, my son, until I see you [again].' So I came to my abode, and I stayed there, and I did according to the command of my holy father, Abba Pisentius.

On the first Sabbath I filled my water-pot with water, and [I took] a little soft wheat, according to the amount which he was likely to eat, according to his command (he gave [me] the order [to bring] two ephahs which he distributed over the forty days), and he took the measure and measured it, saying, 'When you come on the Saturday bring me this measure [full] with the water.' So I took the pitcher of water and the little soft wheat, and I went to the place where he reposed and prayed. And when I had come in to the abode I heard someone weeping and beseeching my father in great tribulation, saying, 'I beseech you, O my lord and father, to pray to the Lord for me so that I may be delivered from these punishments, and that they may never take hold of me again, for I have suffered exceedingly.' I thought that it was a man who was speaking with my father, for the place was in darkness. I sat down, and I perceived the voice of my father, with whom a mummy was speaking. My father said to the mummy, 'What nome do you belong to?' And the mummy said, 'I am from the city of Ermant.' My father said to him, 'Who is your father?' He said, 'My father was Agrikolaos and my mother was Eustathia.' My father said to him, 'Whom did they worship?' And he said, 'They worshipped him who is in the waters, that is to say Poseidôn.' My father said to him, 'Did you not hear before you died that Christ had come into the world?' He said, 'No, my father. My parents were Hellenes, and I followed their life. Woe, woe is me that I was born into the world! Why didn't the womb of my mother become my grave? And it came to pass that when I came into the straits of death, the first who came round about me were the beings "Kosmokrator", and they declared all the evil things which I had done, and they said to me, "Let them come now and deliver you from the punishments where they will cast you." There were iron knives in their hands, and iron daggers with pointed ends as sharp as spear points, and they drove these into my sides, and they gnashed their teeth furiously against me. After a little time my eyes were opened, and I saw death suspended in the air in many forms. Straightway the Angels of cruelty snatched my wretched soul from my body, and they bound it under the form of a black horse, and dragged me to Ement (Amenti). O woe be to every sinner like myself who is born into the world! O my lord and father, they delivered me over into the hands of a large number of tormentors who were merciless, each one of whom had a different form. O how many were the wild beasts which I saw on the road! O how many were the Powers which tortured me! When they had cast me into the outer darkness I saw a great gulf, which was more than a hundred cubits deep, and it was filled with reptiles, and each one of these had seven heads, and all their bodies were covered as it were with scorpions. There was another mighty serpent in that place, and it was exceedingly large, and it was a terrible sight to behold; and it had in its mouth teeth which were like pegs of iron. One laid hold of me and cast me into the mouth of that Worm, which never stopped devouring; all the wild beasts were gathered together about him at all times, and when he filled his mouth all the wild beasts which were round about him filled their mouths with him.'

My father said to him, 'From the time when you died until this day, has no rest been given to you, or have you not been permitted to enjoy any respite from your suffering?' And the mummy said, 'Yes, my father, mercy is shown to those who are suffering torments each Sabbath and each Lord's Day. When the Lord's Day comes to an end, they cast us again into our tortures in order to make us forget the years which we lived in the world. Afterwards, when we have forgotten the misery of this kind of torture, they cast us into another which is far more severe. When you prayed for me, straightway the Lord commanded those who were flogging me, and they removed from my mouth the iron gag which they had placed there, and they released me, and I came to you. Behold, I have told you the conditions under which I subsist. O my lord and father, pray for me, so that they may give me a little rest, and that they may not take me back into that place again.' And my father said to him, 'The Lord is compassionate, and He will show mercy to you. Go back and lie down until the Day of the General Resurrection, where every man shall rise up, and you yourself shall rise with them.' God is my witness, O my brethren, I saw the mummy with my own eyes lie down again in its place, as it was before. Having seen these things I marvelled greatly, and I gave glory to God. And I cried out in front of me, according to the rule, 'Bless me,' and then I went in and kissed his hands and his feet. He said to me, 'John, have you been here a long time? Did you not see somebody or hear somebody talking to me?' And I said, 'No, my father.' He said to me, 'You speak falsehood, just as Gehazi did when he uttered falsehood to the prophet, saying, "Your servant went nowhere." But since you have seen and heard, if you tell any man during my lifetime you shall be cast forth (i.e. excommunicated). And I have observed the order, and I have never dared to repeat it to this very day.

HAVING A DESIRE TO DEPART TO BE WITH CHRIST

It came to pass that God wished to remove him [from this world] to the habitation of those who rejoice, the place where sorrow, and grief, and sighing have fled away, the place where the Prophets and the Patriarchs and the Apostles are, for he was a Patriarch like Abraham, and an Apostle like unto the Apostles, and a Prophet like unto the Prophets, even like unto Samuel, and those who came after him, and he was a high priest [worthy of] reverence, even as were Moses and Aaron and those who came after them.

When he had come to the end of the sickness through which he went to his rest, now it was in the month of Epêp of the fifth year, he cried out to me on the night of the eighth day of Epêp, and he said, 'John, is there anyone with you?' And I said, 'There is no one with me except Moses, and Elisha the Elder, who have come to visit you.' My father cried out, 'Moses, Moses, Moses. Be careful to make your life exceedingly correct. You know in what manner you have been brought up by me. Take great care of my parchment books, for you will have great need for them. And you shall not escape from this burden.' Again he turned to Elisha the Presbyter, and said to him, Elisha, 'Govern most carefully the brethren. Lay fast hold upon the things which I have commanded you, and be sure to summon the brethren regularly each hour in order that they may recite their offices according to the rules of the brethren, and do good to their souls.'

Then Elisha answered and said to him, 'My father, I have approached [the time] for going to all my fathers. If you are going to die it is better that I should die first, for if the pillar in which we are all firmly established shall fall, the destruction of the mountain of Tsentei will draw near. And where shall we find another who will shepherd us as you have done, O my lord and holy father, if you indeed depart? You have directed and made straight the course of your ship to the haven which is fair. You have prepared yourself, and you shall never be disturbed (or, troubled), according to the words of David, [who said,] 'I have set the Lord always before me; because He is at my right hand I shall not be moved (or, troubled).' For we shall feel the lack of you sorely, and we shall be orphans from this day forward.' My father answered and said to me, 'Verily, five days were given to me from the third day.' And I answered and said to him, 'What was it that happened to you that you say these things to me?' And he said to me, 'Before I spoke to you an ecstasy came upon me, and a man of light came and stood before me. And he said to me, "Pisentius, Pisentius, Pisentius" - three times – "prepare yourself, for there remains to you in this world five days, and then you shall come to me." And when he had said these things to me, he departed. And now, behold, I must depart the way of all my fathers.'

When my father had said these things to me, a great outcry broke forth with tears and sobs in [our] midst; 'Thus we are bereaved of our good father, the consoler of those who were in trouble, who gave penitence to the sinner, who provided the poor with food, and who made it his care to find clothing for their bodies.' And I confess to you, [O my beloved], here in the presence of God, that from the time when my father heard concerning the Persians, he never applied to his own use any of the things which could be of use to the poor, even to the cap upon his head, but he distributed everything, and gave it in alms to the poor. The things which he gave with his own hands, and the things which he commanded me to give, and the things which he sent to the faithful, village by village, and which were distributed to each man according to his need, no man can possibly know the sum of them. Only God, to whom all praise be given, knows it.

I said to my holy father, who arrayed himself in Christ, Apa Pisentius, 'Perhaps, O my father, do you think that we shall not again devote ourselves [to the poor], if you do not leave any possessions which may remain to us?' My father answered and said to me, 'We must devote ourselves to the will of God, O my son, and whatsoever you give – everything – to the poor, the Lord will give to us twofold'

What can I say [more], or what can I relate of the valiant deeds of this just man? But now let us devote ourselves to the consideration of his laying down of the body. Now he passed three days where he neither ate nor drank, neither did he speak to us, nor turn from one side to the other, but he lay stretched out like a dead man in the hall of the large cell. Then he cried out, 'John,' and I answered, 'Bless me.' He said to me, 'I have come near to my departure, and I shall finish my course at the time when the sun shall set tomorrow, which shall be the thirteenth day. But take good heed and do not permit any man to carry my body away from the place which shall be dug for it. During these three days which I have just passed where I held no conversation with you, I have been standing in the presence of God, and my speech has been taken away since the ninth hour yesterday. I tell you that God will show His mercy to me.'

I said to him, 'Do one act of grace, O my father, and partake of a very small quantity of nourishment, for behold, it is now four days since you have tasted anything at all.' My father answered and said to me, 'My son, shall I eat anything else after [this] word? I say that I will not taste any food whatsoever belonging to this world, and I shall eat nothing at all until I depart to the Christ, and break my fast with Him.' And it came to pass that when the light had risen on the thirteenth day of the month Epêp, he said to me – now there were also certain great men sitting by him – 'John, you know all my affairs, and that I have nothing left belonging to the bishopric [or] to the town of Kebt (Coptos) with which to bury my body. Nevertheless, I had one good "holokottinos" by me, which I had kept since the day when I lived a life of contemplation in my cell and when I was a monk. This I made to yield an increase through the work of my hands, and I have guarded it carefully until the day where I should have to clothe my body with the work of my hands, so that I might not leave behind me a matter of unpleasantness for those who should succeed me, and who would say, You have broken a custom which was seemly. Do then, O John, buy a covering for my body, and do not put on me anything except the shroud with which I am wrapped, and my monk's dress, and my skull-cap, and my girdle, and my tunic only these- and you shall prepare me for burial and you shall bury me. And I think, Behold a garden where they will bury me. And behold, a place full of wolves, but they will throw a wall about [me], each one working at it according to his good pleasure. But whatever each man does, let no man rebuke him, saying, The wall must be thrown round [the grave].'

When the holy father Apa Pisentius, the holy bishop, had said these things, he cried out to us, and spoke words to [each] one of us, and then he opened his mouth, and yielded up his spirit into the hands of God, at the moment when the sun was about to set on the thirteenth day of the month of Epêp of this fifth year [of the Indiction]. And we lifted up his holy coffin, and we took it into the holy chamber of the altar of the congregation of Tsentei, and we made it ready for burial according to the instructions which he had given us, and we passed the whole night in lamentation for him. Afterwards we partook of the Holy Offering over him, and we carried him away into the mountain to the place which he had made us dig for him that he might remain in our neighbourhood. We buried him on the fourteenth day of this same month Epêp. In the Peace of God. Amen.

www.ingramcontent.com/pod-product-compliance
Lightning Source LLC
LaVergne TN
LVHW091309080426
835510LV00007B/433